Wedding Planning Survival Guide

TEM Publishing

ISBN:1468127314
ISBN-13: 978-1468127317

DEDICATION

This book is dedicated to all of the incredible professionals and companies who took the time to submit content to this book. It has been a pleasure working with each of you, on the production of this book. The time you have all taken and the quality content that you have all shared has truly gone above and beyond anything we could have ever expected when we first set out to publish this book. Thank you to everyone who made this possible.

CONTENTS

Introduction   1

1   Choosing the Right Wedding Planner   Pg 5

2   Finding a Professional Photographer   Pg 11

3   Wedding Party Rental and Service Staff   Pg 19

4   What to Look for When Selecting a Florist for Your Wedding   Pg 27

5   Tips for Finding the Best Cake Specialist for Your Wedding   Pg 33

6   Facts You Should Know before Purchasing a Bridal Gown   Pg 37

7   How to Hire a Great DJ for Your Wedding   Pg 45

8   Finding the Right Hairstylist for Your Big Day   Pg 53

9   Choosing an Experienced Makeup Artist   Pg 57

10   Honeymoon Travel Booking!   Pg 65

A Vacation That Should Never Be Forgotten

Conclusion   Pg 101

NOTES

INTRODUCTION

Thank you for purchasing Wedding Planning Survival Guide. When we set out to publish this book, it was our goal to obtain real world, usable advice, from true industry experts. We are proud and excited to tell you that we have greatly exceeded even our own high expectations, in this regard.

Wedding Planning Survival Guide is truly a compilation of the information that you absolutely must have before you embark on the massive task of planning your own wedding. Our interviewees have shared their knowledge and expertise, to help your wedding go off without a hitch.

Very often, in books that are written in this interview style, you'll find interviews with professionals who are mainly just interested in promoting their own companies. We are pleased to let you know that the contributors of this book have truly put your interests ahead of their own. As you'll see, from reading these interviews, each of our contributors shares exactly what you need to do and what you need to avoid doing when you're planning your wedding.

Weddings can often be the subject of funny stories...for the guests. These same "funny stories", however, are usually nightmares or unpleasant events for the bride and groom. In the great majority of cases, these unpleasant incidences could have been avoided if the bride and groom had just a little bit of "insider knowledge" when they were planning their wedding. The very nature of most weddings, however, is that it's a first-time and often one-time event, where there are no second chances. The best strategy for getting it right the first time, therefore, is to learn from the experts who have years of experience in the wedding industry.

After you read this book, you're going to have insights and knowledge that has taken years for our interviewees to acquire. Very often, married couples will look back on their wedding day, wishing they had done certain things differently. After reading this book, the likelihood of you having those same regrets will be greatly diminished. Your wedding is truly a milestone event in your life and we set out to ensure that you get it right the first time, because hopefully, there won't be a second time! After reading this book, we genuinely believe that you will feel confident to plan your wedding with enthusiasm and certainty. So, without further ado, let's get into the interviews!

NOTES

CHAPTER 1

Choosing the Right Wedding Planner

Featuring an Interview with Glenna of "Memory Makers Event Planning"

Memory Makers Event Planning, LLC plans and coordinates events to be held in southwestern Idaho and eastern Oregon. We specialize in weddings, receptions and other family events, as well as planning and coordinating events for small and mid-sized businesses, non-profits and government agencies. We plan unique events that reflect your personality and tastes while keeping your budget in mind.

What are the main functions and responsibilities of a Wedding Planner?

There are two types of wedding planners. The first helps with all the planning, including helping a couple find just the right venue and the right combination of merchants to create a wedding that reflects the couple's personalities and tastes. The planner recommends merchants and goes with the bride or the couple to meet with them. The planner helps the couple create a master plan for the day and she/he is there for the rehearsal and the wedding day. She/he meets merchants when they arrive, makes sure everything is set up correctly and generally keeps the event running smoothly.

The second type is more often called a wedding coordinator. This is the person who steps in after the couple has completed their planning and manages their wedding rehearsal and wedding day for them. She should help the couple create a master plan and be there for the rehearsal and the wedding day to oversee merchant arrivals and all necessary set-up.

What are the advantages of hiring a Wedding Planner, as opposed to a couple planning their own wedding?

There are numerous advantages to hiring a wedding planner. First, she/he knows the local market. She can eliminate countless hours of phone calls and visits by recommending the right combination of merchants to fit the wedding location and the couple's tastes and budgets. Second, the bride or groom can't do everything on the wedding day. There are hair appointments, photos and other commitments that preclude the bride from setting up tables/meeting vendors/lighting candles and all the myriad details that a planner handles. When there is no planner, the mother of the bride or groom is often the one rushing around in the background, and who may not be able to enjoy her guests on the big day.

After hiring a Wedding Planner, can the couple, as well as friends and family still help in planning the wedding?

A good planner should carry out the wishes of the couple. That means constant involvement on their part. The planner should not make decisions for the couple without their in-put unless it is a last minute decision made on the wedding day to prevent something from happening, such as a cake collapsing. Though family involvement is encouraged, the couple should make the final decisions, not a mother, step-mother or someone else who may try to take control of the wedding.

Is it a good idea for a couple to hire a Wedding Planner if they don't like being told what to do?

A good wedding planner will recommend, not tell. Occasionally I will have a person, usually a groom, who is unfamiliar with the requirements of the wedding venue or of a particular merchant and who doesn't like being told that he can't do something, such as bring his own alcohol into a facility that has an on-site alcohol license. Usually, when the situation is explained, the person understands and complies.

What can a Wedding Planner offer that wedding planning books and wedding planning software cannot provide?

A wedding planner knows the merchants in the community. She/he knows who provides a quality product at a reasonable price and who offers the best customer service. She/he can sometimes save the couple the cost of her services by helping them make wise choices. A wedding planner is there to answer questions, take care of details and calm frazzled nerves - something a book or software usually can't do.

If a couple is on a tight budget, can they afford a Wedding Planner?

You get what you pay for, so a couple shouldn't choose the least expensive planner if that person lacks experience or they are not comfortable with the person's personality. In most cases, a couple hires a planner several months before their wedding. That allows time for them to make payments if necessary. They may also be able to pay the planner a lower fee if the planner provides merchant referrals but does not go with the couple to merchant meetings, which can take quite a bit of time. Often, because of her knowledge of the market, a planner can save the couple money by helping them make the best choices for their limited funds.

How much money should a couple set aside for the services of a Wedding Planner?

It depends on where the couple lives. In most areas of the country, planners charge a flat fee. In large metropolitan areas planners may charge a percentage of the couple's budget. Generally, a couple should plan on paying from $500 to $1,000, depending on the scope of services desired.

What should a couple look for in a good Wedding Planner?

Experience is key. Find out how long the planner has been in business; how many weddings they have planned; what venues has she worked at. Ask to see photos of past events. Secondly, personality is important. A good planner should be knowledgeable yet not try to take charge. She/he should work well with other merchants, such as caterers, photographers and DJs. You don't want a planner who will try to be the life of the party but rather one who will work in the background without drawing attention to himself/herself. The planner should become your friend during the months leading up to the wedding.

What should a couple look out for when selecting a Wedding Planner?

Beware of the person who just opened their doors. They may not know what they are doing; they may not have the contacts in the community to create a well-planned event. Nationwide, the average wedding/event planner stays in business less than two years. Therefore, ask how long the person has been in business; ask for references and check them. Talk with your caterer, photographer and other merchants and ask about the person. Check them out online, both their web site and by Googling their name and their business name. That way, you may find customer reviews and customer rants. Beware of anyone who is too aggressive or pushy.

If a couple will be getting married in a location that is far away from where they live, should they hire a Wedding Planner that is close to where they live or close to where their wedding will be?

Please explain why one of these options would be better than the other.

They should hire a planner who lives close to the location where the wedding will occur. That person will be familiar with the local market and be able to help them secure all the services they need, including a venue. A local planner can do the "leg work" for them, picking up menus and contracts and other items. The planner will be familiar with state laws (including alcohol laws), city and county regulations (such as noise ordinances), and other things that could impact their event. Today, with email, scanning, and phone calls, it is easy to plan a wedding from a distance with the assistance of a local planner.

Memory Makers Event Planning, LLC
www.memorable-events.com
http://mainevent.blogspot.com
event@memorable-events.com

NOTES

CHAPTER 2

FINDING
A PROFESSIONAL PHOTOGRAGHER

Featuring an Interview with Professional Photographer
Julian Jenkins of "Jenkins Photography"

Julian Jenkins has been capturing images for over twenty-five years and was educated in the field of photojournalism while living in Los Angeles where he worked for various newspapers and publications in the Los Angeles beach cities area of El Segundo, Manhattan Beach, Redondo Beach, Torrance, Inglewood and Hawthorne. In 1996, he started shooting weddings professionally. He currently lives and works in the Boise, Idaho area.

What are the advantages of hiring a professional wedding photographer as opposed to having a friend or family member take the pictures?

One bride told me what she was purchasing was piece of mind. I thought that was very important to mention to brides in the future. It really is exactly that, knowing you are in good hands and that your images will be done to the best standards of a professional. A professional wants repeat business, referrals to friends or guests at the wedding is a vital part of the business. A friend or family member should be there as a guest, not a working vendor. If the images turn out badly, is the bride going to complain to that loved one about the lousy (probably free or low cost) job they did? Chances are, no, they won't as it could start a family feud that would go on for years. A wonderful wedding coordinator once told me, and I quote, "The bitter taste of poor quality lingers long after the bargain price has been forgotten."

Why do wedding photographers copyright the pictures they take at weddings? Is this common?

Copyright is actually in place the moment the photographer releases the shutter button. Real professionals tend to keep their copyrights to all images they take, period. They will in some cases offer packages that include some client printing rights or licensing of rights. Printing rights is the right to print some or all of the wedding images for personal use only. All commercial and other rights are usually held by the photographer. They have simply licensed the images from the wedding to you for personal use.

Is it better to book a wedding photographer who uses film or digital equipment?

The debate will rage on I'm sure, but in the days when digital cameras took two megapixel images I'd say film was king. Now in 2011, those days are, for the most part, over. Higher megapixel counts in digital single lens reflex cameras (DSLR cameras) have taken us well into the depth and clarity that high end film cameras like medium format or large format would bring us in the past. For some "looks" you can't beat film still, but the associated costs are generally prohibitive to the average wedding client. If needed, software like Photoshop can achieve the same vintage feel that film used to offer.

What is a proof and what are the advantages of the different types of proofing?

Proofs are what was called a "proof sheet" (many smaller photos on a 8x10 photo sheet or the more expensive single image proofs, usually a 4x6 or slightly larger.) The proofs are meant for the bride and groom to look through and find their favorites that they wanted to commit to seeing printed. Now with the advent of the internet, you can "proof" the images online for a nominal fee or sometimes free. (Web space does cost money so don't be surprised if a $5 to $25 online proof fee is charged. Understanding that wedding proofs would cost hundreds to print, that's quite a savings.

What are the pros and cons of hiring two wedding photographers to take pictures at a wedding, as

compared to only having one photographer taking pictures?

Depending on the size of the wedding, two photographers are needed just for the sake of having two professionals (at different angles) capturing all the key moments like the kiss, first dance, cake cutting, etc. The difference in one photographer covering a 60 guest wedding compared to a 300 guest wedding is huge. The size of the location and how your wedding timeline can also point to whether you need multiple photographers. If the groom and bride are getting ready in different locations, one person can't be in two places at one time. Don't skimp, hire two pros if in doubt.

What types of wedding packages do photographers typically offer?

Packages will very per photographer and the region they shoot in. Pricing all depends on time the photographer is working the wedding, final products ordered (prints, wedding books, etc) and other factors like travel, lodging, etc.

What is the customary deposit to put down, to reserve a photographer for a date? When is the balance typically due?

Deposits, or down payments, are usually half the total amount and due when you'd like to secure the date. Having been in business for years, I've found that having the clients pay the balance 30 days before the event is easier than billing the amount after the wedding. Some photographers have the balance due when the proofs are available to view which is usually a month or so after the wedding.

Why is there such a large price range among different wedding photographers?

People tend to charge what they feel they are worth. Of course there are regional demographics that come into play. Moving from Los Angeles, California to Boise, Idaho there was a big difference in pricing. It was at least a 1/3 less in Idaho. The shorter shooting season is also a factor. In cold weather climates the wedding season could be quite a bit shorter than say Florida, or the west coast states. The fact that many people have joined the ranks of wedding photographers with digital photography becoming more available to the populace cannot be overlooked. Many of these folks have no real education in the art but have found it a "fun" way to make some extra money for their family. Looker deeper into their portfolio should separate the pros from the novices. Having a greatest hits web page of photos compared to a body of work that looks professional is one avenue of shopping for your photographer.

At what point in the wedding planning process should a couple book a wedding photographer?

Most areas the booking window is at least a year or more in advance to secure the talent you want. That time can vary but it's a good rule of thumb. Better to book talent you want rather then less talent because you are stuck one month before the big day. The planning of the whole affair usually takes 12-18 months so a photographer should be looked at early in the process. As well, engagement sessions happen fairly quickly after the question is popped.

What should a couple look for in a wedding photographer?

Simply said, the images and photographer have to connect with you. The images should be well exposed, composed and interesting to the bride and groom. Tons of gimmicky angles like tilted horizons or over toned prints could mean the photographer is over compensating for lack of photography skills or schooling in the art.

What should a couple beware of with certain wedding photographers?

Lack of professionalism is usually easy to spot. A disconnected "hello" when you call the first time, dogs barking or kids crying in the background could show that the photographer is not doing the job for a living. In fact, you interrupted their normal day of noise. That could lead to a "it's good enough" attitude and images that are not what you expected or paid for. Lots of "wedding photographers" are flooding the market in most areas. Be cautious, look for signs of someone hoping to start a business rather than having a business. In the final analysis, it's the biggest day of your life short the birth of any children you'll have, don't risk it.

How should a couple determine their wedding photography budget?

Budgeting is always a tough call. It would be nice if we all just had unlimited funds but bride and grooms are trying to get the most bang for their collective buck. Look at your needs and wants and define the two. What you "need" is sometimes not what you "want." Look at the budget as a realist, and get the best vendor you can afford.

What equipment should a wedding photographer have?

Pro level gear should be the standard for a true professional. Basic DSLRs with plastic "kit" lens (the kind you get for free when you buy the camera at a big box store) is not the hallmark of a pro. Professional quality gear usually shows

the photographer has arrived to a level that most consumers can't or won't invest in. It's hard to know what's professional equipment wise, but just the photographer having a black camera with a long lens is not a way to tell. If you're wondering, ask them! Most photographers are gear heads and like talking equipment. Take note and look it up. There are huge differences in say, a Canon Rebel to their Canon 1D series cameras.

Do prices typically vary for off-season or weekday weddings?

Some companies, as mine, offer discounts on off-season days or weekday weddings. It just depends. It never hurts to ask, most professionals are glad to talk pricing with you. As well, some will offer discounts for veterans.

Is it possible to get black and white photographs as well as color photographs, or do couples typically have to decide between one or the other?

If your photographer is shooting film still you will have to ask for one or the other, or a combination of both. With digital images taken with today's cameras, all images are shoot in color but with some software post production can be flipped to black and white. It is not as simple as using a simple software to create a black and white (thus a gray) image. A true black and white will be just that, tuxes are black, bride's dress is white.

Julian D. Jenkins
Jenkins Photography
PO Box 414
Meridian, Idaho 83680
208-887-6655
www.jenkinsphoto.com
boiseweddings@gmail.com

CHAPTER 3

Wedding Party Rental & Service Staff

Featuring an Interview with Kongmeng Tang of "Blissful Events & Weddings"

Blissful Events & Weddings is an event and wedding planning &; decorating team that provides full service planning and hands on support. Our focused design, detailed plans, and seamless execution will provide a memorable event for you and your guests. Our specialty is ceiling and wall draping. Other services we provide are planning &; coordinating, event lighting, linen rentals, specialty linen rentals, floral bouquet/pieces, centerpieces, décor design and set up as well as wedding invitations. Ka Yang-Owner/Certified Wedding Planner-Designer www.ourblissevents.com ka@ourblissevents.com 414.405.5463

How do party rental companies ensure that equipment is only provided at the exact time of the ceremony and/or reception?

Rental companies will normally contact the venue to arrange times that will work out for both the venue &; rental company. In the case that there is a wedding planner, the wedding planner may also arrange this so that everything is in place. Depending which rental company you go to, it would be good to confirm with the rental company whether the are contacting the venue or if you are to supply them with that information.

Do party rental companies usually have a minimum order size for delivery?

There is usually a minimum order in regards to quantity or in dollar amount. Some rental companies will charge a delivery fee in lieu of the minimum order. A majority of rental companies do charge a delivery fee no matter how large the order is. It also will depend on the type of equipment or product you are renting. For example, if you are renting out a lighting system, some rental companies require you to pay a fee to have one of their people work the lighting system, even if you can work it yourself. This is to protect the equipment so that it is not misused.

What if a couple needs more equipment after a delivery has already been made?

Rental companies will usually have an event manager who will help you book all the items that are needed for your wedding. This event manager will usually give out their phone number in the case that there is an emergency. If the items are delivered a few days in advance, it would be good to contact the event manager, but not necessarily. Contacting the rental company and checking for availability with anyone there should be fine. If it is within the same day or after hours, I would contact the event manager since this would be more of an event emergency than anything else.

What should a couple do if they did not receive all of the equipment they ordered or if they are not happy with the condition of the equipment?

They should contact the event manager. This should be the person who booked everything for your wedding event. If they are not available, contact the rental company. If there is no response, be sure to document the attempts and call when they are open. They should issue a partial refund if it is their error. It would be a good idea to see the equipment first. Some couples don't really care as long as the equipment is working and decent in presentation. Others are very detailed and want everything perfect, so it is good to express your thoughts to the event manager when booking the rental.

Also keep in mind that these are rental items so they may not look brand new, but should be clean, working, and presentable.

What if a couple needs to contact their party rental company, in an emergency, after normal business hours?

They should contact the Event Manager. They usually will provide a cell phone for emergencies. Some rental companies should have an after hours number to call, but with my experience, there is usually an event manager who will give you an emergency contact to themselves or to someone who can page them. This is also a good question to ask a rental company you are wanting to book. Not expecting that a crisis may arise, but you want to make sure the company you are booking for your wedding is going to be as flexible as possible and cater to your needs. There are some companies who don't give out after hours/emergency numbers, if that is the case, this may be something you want to re-evaluate. If it is more affordable, you have the risk of "What if?". I would compare apples to apples when it comes to vendors for your wedding. One may have the same item and be $10 cheaper, but if they do not offer services that cater to your needs, it may be worth it to go with the vendor who is focused on customer service and not just pricing.

Who typically sets up the equipment?

For event rental companies, they will have workers or they themselves will set up. That way the equipment is properly handled and not damaged by others who may not know how to handle the equipment, but this is normally for an additional fee. If the equipment is something that is not hard to set up such as tables, chairs, etc, the customer may choose to set up themselves, they won't charge a set up fee with this option, but may charge a damage waiver fee.

What should be done with dishware, flatware and glassware before it is returned?

It is asked that the dishes be returned with no chunks of food on the dishware, flatware, and glassware. There is no need to do a thorough wash, but to get chunks of food off would help. You don't want to return the plates with a half eaten steak. Depending how long it takes for you to return your dishes, you wouldn't want to return a pile of foul odor plates because the food was not thrown away.

What do you suggest a couple does if they need to keep equipment longer than originally planned?

It would be good to contact the rental company. Contact the company the morning you are suppose to return it so they can look it up to make sure it is okay. Depending on each rental company, they may stock multiple items of the same product. They could have the product rented out to another customer, so it would be good to double check first. Be aware that they can and will charge either a late fee for not returning it in time or charge you for another day (or as long as you need it).

How can couples typically see the equipment they're think about renting ahead of time?

If the event rental company has multiple equipment, then the best would be to visit the showroom. If that is not possible, the event rental company may invite you to a wedding they are doing so you can see the equipment first hand. If neither is possible, I would ask the rental company to send you a recent picture of it, via email so you can see it.

Do party rental companies usually deliver the equipment or is it normally picked up?

It depends on each company, but they will deliver if the customer pays a delivery fee. If the customer does not want to pay the delivery fee, they can opt to pick up the equipment themselves. Depending on what items are rented, the rental company may require they deliver and set up only so the equipment does not get damaged. An example would be if a customer rented a stage. Not many people would know how to set up a stage & it can be damaged, so the rental company may ask you to pay a set up fee for this since it is not something a customer can normally set up.

With regard to having equipment available for weddings that are during off-hours, how is that normally handled?

As a customer, you want to make sure you have an emergency contact for the company in the case something goes wrong. Usually the event manager for the rental company will give out their number so they can handle anything that may come up after normal business hours.

Do party rental companies typically do deliveries and/or pickups on Sundays or holidays?

Usually rental companies do not deliver or pick up on Sundays or holidays, unless it is arranged and in the contract. If your wedding is on a Sunday or Holiday and needs delivery, it would be good to have it written in the contract so that you are guaranteed that delivery, if not they may not honor your verbal agreement. If the equipment or product is available a few days before the event, they may be able to deliver a day or two in advance and pick up a day or two after the wedding if needed.

website: www.ourblissevents.com
email: ka@ourblissevents.com
phone: 414.405.5463

NOTES

CHAPTER 4

WHAT TO LOOK FOR WHEN SELECTING A FLORIST FOR YOUR WEDDING

Florist Lisa Anderson of "Sweet Pea Flowers" Shares Her Professional Input

What should couples be aware of when selecting a florist for their big day?

Couples should ask their potential florist: How many years experience they have, how many events in a weekend they do, what is their style (to ensure that the florist is flexible enough to work with all ranges of styles), and will the same person that designs my wedding actually be working on my wedding.

What are some simple things that a couple can do to ensure that their flowers are consistent with what they visualize for their wedding?

Keep in mind your budget and ask the florist honestly if what you envision is possible within that budget, request a green house visit with the florist, ask for photos of work that is similar to what the couple is envisioning, request a mock up(just keep in mind mock ups generally cost extra), keep in contact with your florist throughout the process-making sure that you email the florist to let them know of any concrete changes that have been made so everyone stays on the same page throughout.

Can Wedding bouquets be customized or can only certain flowers be used in bouquets?

Anything and everything can be accommodated for a bouquet. Just keep in mind, flowers are seasonal items, so it may be harder or more expensive to acquire out of season flowers, make sure to discuss this option with your florist.

What is the customary process for placing deposits and paying the remaining balance?

Generally, you will place a percentage of the subtotal (that varies from florist to florist, and can be anywhere from 30% to 50%) down for your deposit in order for your florist to hold the date for you. Keep in mind, the deposit confirms and holds the date for you, the client, and generally ensures that the florist won't take on any other events after you have booked. After the deposit and contract are received by the florist, general practice is that the remaining balance will be required one month to two weeks prior to the event date.

What is the difference between a ladies buttonhole and a corsage?

A ladies buttonhole is generally a smaller version of a corsage, and it is pinned onto the blouse or lapel of whatever she is wearing. A corsage is larger and is worn on the wrist. If neither is appealing to the couple, a smaller version of the bouquet, commonly referred to as a posy or nosegay, is on the rise in popularity.

Are the flowers for the ceremony and the wedding reception two separate orders or are they typically all ordered as one package?

How far in advance should couples order their wedding flowers?

Generally, all the flowers needed are ordered as one big order. Speak to your florist though, to make sure this is the case as all floral design companies are different. Typically, your floral orders should be placed six to eight months prior to your event. This allows plenty of time for meeting the florist, ensuring the date, and having flexibility to work with the florist in designing your dream wedding.

Considering that weddings take place on specific times and dates, how can a couple ensure that wedding flowers are delivered at the right time, for the ceremony and the reception?

Ensuring that your florist has the timeline of events for the wedding day is the top way to ensure timely delivery and set-up. Making sure that you communicate with all your vendors, including the florist, what time they need to be there, how long they have to set up, any special provisions to the set-up process and any movement of items that is needed (i.e. moving objects from the ceremony site to the reception site) is another key to making sure your wedding day runs as smoothly as possible.

Is it fairly common for couples to meet with the florist prior to their wedding? If so, what should a couple bring with them to a consultation?

Yes, that is a very important part of the planning process. It is the best way for you, the couple to get to know your florist and make sure you have good working chemistry with them. It is also the best way to ensure you get what you want, and that you are working with a reputable company. You should bring color swatches, photographs, and any questions you may come up with. The more the florist knows about you and your style, the better prepared they are, which means you will have a more productive meeting.

Approximately how much should a couple budget for their flowers, in proportion to their entire wedding budget?

The general rule of thumb is 10%-20% of your entire wedding budget should go to flowers. It really does depend though on how important certain aspects of your day are to you. If flowers are the most important thing to your day, than that percent can go up. Alternately, if flowers are not the most important part of your day, than stick closer to 10% of your overall budget.

Is it true that flower prices fluctuate throughout the year? If so, by how much do these prices fluctuate?

Yes, that is true. It all really depends though on how much they fluctuate. The variables are the season, the weather where the flowers are grown, and the rarity of the flower. If you want a peony in July, they will be more expensive and not as big(and may not even be available) because the growing season starts in November for those types of flowers and goes until June. Also, if there is a natural disaster of any kind where the flowers are grown, that will really affect the price of the flowers. Your florist should be knowledgeable enough to know when the flowers you are requesting are available and if the price is too high.

Sweet Pea Flowers
3563 Larimer St.
Suite A
Denver, CO 80205
www.sweetpea-flowers.com

CHAPTER 5

TIPS FOR FINDING THE BEST CAKE SPECIALIST FOR YOUR WEDDING

An Interview with the "Vermont Cake Studio"

Vermont Cake Studio is a boutique cakery located in Central Vermont. Our goal is to create a delicious and unique work of art that will be the centerpiece of your celebration. We really enjoy what we do here at Vermont Cake Studio and enjoy sharing that passion with our clients!
Vermont Cake Studio 2007 Guptil Road Waterbury VT 05677 802 244-5151
www.vermontcakestudio.com

How long, before the big day, should a wedding cake be ordered?

6 months to a year ahead is usually best. When we get into the heart of the wedding season our schedule is very tight and it is hard for us to give the undivided attention you and your cake deserve!

What are some factors that determine the various prices of wedding cakes?

Ingredients and finish work. We bake everything from scratch and use high quality ingredients like Vermont Butter, Belgian Chocolate, and Pure Maple Syrup. There are no preservatives in our cakes and nothing comes out of a can. Naturally it costs a bit more but the taste of the finished product is well worth it. Finish work is what happens on the outside of the cake. Handmade sugar flowers or lots of additional piping will add to the cost of your cake.

What are some of the different ingredient and flavor options that can be selected for wedding cakes?

Chocolate Chiffon layered with Truffle Cream, Raspberry Preserves and Hazelnut Praline. Iced with Chambord Butter cream. Harvest Carrot Cake Sandwiched with Maple Infused Cream Cheese Icing. Lemon Poppy Pound Cake Layered with Blueberry Preserves, Lemon Mascarpone Cream, and Fresh Blueberries. Iced with limoncello Buttercream.

Do wedding cake bakers generally allow couples to sample cakes before ordering them? If yes, is there usually a cost for this?

Yes tastings are quite popular. We charge for our tastings because we make two individual cakes for each couple to try. We don't keep any of our cakes or fillings frozen, ever. Each cake is a unique creation.

Can special instructions/arrangements usually be made to account for people with certain food allergies?

Yes, we make nut free and gluten free cakes all the time.

If there are pre-arranged flowers, that need to be placed on a cake, who normally does this?

We do all of our own flower work on our cakes to ensure that the cake we envisioned with our clients is realized.

Do wedding cakes usually include a cake topper, or is this ordered separately?

It is ordered separately unless the cake topper is made in house. We have made sugar paste figurines, monograms, and snowflakes to name a few.

Who normally puts the cake topper on a wedding cake and when is this done?

We do and it is done at delivery 1-2 hrs prior to the ceremony.

What if more people will be attending the wedding than was originally expected? What can be done to ensure that there will be enough cake for these extra guests?

The final guest count is due one month prior to the wedding so surprises are unusual. Our cakes have ample proportions for all of the wedding guests and usually the amount of cake ordered reflects the guest count precisely. We haven't ever run out of cake at an event. However, we do over/under order if our clients express concern. Some families are really not "cake people" and we respect that. Of course we don't really understand it ... :-)

Who is normally responsible for delivering the cake to the reception location?

The pastry chef is usually responsible. We don't normally do pickups unless the cake is very small. Delivery is stressful enough for those of us that do it every week, we have no desire to pass that stress along to our clients.

Is a delivery charge standard on wedding cake orders?

Yes it is.

Vermont Cake Studio 2007 Guptil Road Waterbury VT 05677 802 244-5151
www.vermontcakestudio.com

CHAPTER 6

Facts You Should Know Before Purchasing a Bridal Gown

Interview With

Storybook Bridal is a Bridal Salon located in Northwest Idaho. We cater to all Bride's, Bridesmaids, Flower Girls, and other woman searching for Bridal and Formal wear. We also carry a wide variety of wedding merchandise. Our gowns are chosen to offer you choices to match your personality and style. From traditional, glamorous and romantic to modern, fun and sophisticated. With our help you are sure to make an exquisite statement of style and beauty on your wedding day.

If a bride-to-be sees a gown online or in a magazine, can bridal salons typically get specific brands or styles that they don't usually carry?

Typically a Bridal Salon cannot order from lines they do not have a relationship with. Most designers require that the Salons establish an account which includes a credit check of the owner as well as maintain minimum orders throughout the year. However, a Salon could choose to order such dresses off the black market or knock offs online that come from China. Serious quality issues can arise from these types of orders and the Salon is putting their name at risk.

What is the price range for a bridal gown and what determines this price range?

Bridal gowns come in all price ranges. The Designer, material, amount of embellishments, and type of gown can all contribute to the price of each particular gown. Designers such as Vera Wang and Jim Hjelm have much higher priced gowns while Ella and Jasmine carry lines in more affordable ranges.

How does the process work for ordering a dress and having it ready in time for the big day?

Once a Bride finds her perfect dress the ordering process begins. Measurements are taken along with the color and any changes she wishes to have done and the order is placed with the Designer. During the first part of the year most orders take 3 months to be fulfilled due to the high demand from summer weddings but after the first quarter is complete a rush can be placed on orders and the time can be shortened to 8 weeks.

What are the dress sizes that are available for bridal gowns?

Gown sizes start at 00 and typically go up size 32. There are special designers who cater to even larger sizes although an alteration's specialist can certainly help plus size women who may need an even larger size.

How does a bride-to-be determine which dress size to order?

Once a Bridal Consultant and the Bride has completed the process of selecting the perfect gown measurements are taken to determine the exact size of the Bride. These measurements include the Bust, Waist, Hips, and Hem.

Why would a bride-to-be need to order extra fabric and why is this sometimes requested?

A Bride-to-Be will sometimes order extra fabric that can help when alterations are needed. An Alteration's Specialist can add sizes to a gown if the size needed is not available or not able to be ordered. This happens when a Bride-to be buys a gown off a sale rack where gowns are discontinued and no longer made by that particular Designer. Additional material can also be ordered so a veil or other pieces can be designed to match the gown of choice.

Do bridal gowns come in petite sizes? If so, what are the sizes in this category?

Bridal gowns come in all sizes including petite. Petite sizes normally include sizes 00 (zero zero) up to 6.

What is a "hollow-to-hem" measurement?

The "hollow-to-hem" measurement is a specific measurement that specifies the length of a Bridal gown. This measurement is taken from the depression of the neck just above the collar bone and extends to the hem of the particular dress that is being purchased.

Do bridal gowns only come in white? If not, what are some other colors that a bridal gown can come in and when would a color other than white be appropriate?

Bridal gowns can come in any color but traditionally they are designed in white, ivory, or champagne. A more mature bride might choose to order a gown in a color other than white if they have been married in the past or have children. Some brides might choose to have a colored gown to match a particular theme they have chosen such as a Halloween Wedding where a bride might choose to wear black.

Why would a bride custom order a gown as compared to purchasing one that is already in the store?

Some Brides choose to order a custom gown so that they are the only one to have worn it or to obtain a dress that is part of a current Designer's Line. Dresses that are already in a Bridal Salon will have been tried on by several women looking for their perfect dress. These dresses sometimes experience some abuse causing stains, snags, and other imperfections.

What is a "trunk show"?

A Trunk Show is where a Bridal Salon showcases a particular Designer for a day, week, or weekend and sometimes

includes fashion shows, meet and greets, as well as extra
discounts for any orders placed during the show.

**What is a blusher? Is this something that brides still
wear?**

Blusher is make up that some brides use to add color and
definition to cheek bones. Some brides will use this but it
usually depends on their make-up artist and their style of
art.

**Do veils have to be ordered separately or are they
included with the gown?**

Veils are not included in a gown order. Extra material can be
ordered so a seamstress can design a veil to match the gown
or a veil can be purchased that compliments the gown the
bride has chosen.

What is a bustle?

A bustle is a part of a bridal gown that lifts the train for the
reception after the ceremony is complete. Usually a bustle is
added by an Alteration's Specialist and comes in many
forms. A bride could choose to have the bustle include a

wrist strap where she is required to carry the train or a design that allows the train to tuck up under the gown.

How do brides store their gowns before and after the wedding?

Gowns are usually hung in a garment bag prior to the wedding and steamed just before the big day. After the wedding is over a dry cleaner can clean the dress and perform a process called preservation where the dresses is packed into an air tight box or bag that won't allow harmful elements to alter the quality of the material.

What should a bride-to-be bring to the alteration fitting?

A Bride-to-Be should bring the shoes they are planning to wear the day of her wedding as well as and any under garments that will be worn. Jewelry and other accessories could be useful at this meeting as well. Make-up should be kept to a minimum as you will be putting the gown on and off and you won't want to cause stains or the purpose of cleaning prior to the big day.

What is the customary deposit needed for ordering a gown?

Each bridal salon requires different deposits when placing an order. Normally a 50% deposit is mandatory and the other 50% is required upon picking up the dress when it arrives.

Should a bride-to-be call in advance, to schedule an appointment, if they are coming in for a fitting?

It is a very good idea to schedule an appointment when searching for a bridal gown. Bridal salons will have the opportunity to be prepared for your visit and will usually block out the time for you and hold off other brides who are "walk-ins". Better fitting rooms and the undivided attention of your Bridal Consultant are certainly perks of scheduling your fitting in advance.

Storybook Bridal
1520 Northwest Blvd.
Coeur d'Alene, ID 83814
www.StorybookBridal.com
(208) 765-6900
http://www.facebook.com/#!/pages/Storybook-Bridal/296915250326817

CHAPTER 7

How to Hire a Great DJ for Your Wedding

Interview with "Jammin DJs" of Colorado

JAMMIN' DJs is an award winning DJ Company that specializes in wedding receptions. Not only are we on most venues preferred vendor lists, we received:

2007 "Best of Weddings" by The Knot Magazine,

2008 TOP 3 Entertainment Companies by Denver's Channel 7 A-List!

2009 Accredited A+ Rated business by the BBB!

2009 Top 5 Entertainment Companies by Denver's Channel 7 A-List!

2010 "Best of Weddings" by The Knot Magazine!

2010 Brides Choice Award" – Weddingwire.com

2010 Top 5 Entertainment Companies by Denver's Channel 7 A-List!

2010 "Best of Entertainment" - onewed.com

2011 "Brides Choice Award" - Weddingwire.com You can also view our wedding demo DVD: youtube.com/watch popup?v=YEbY gHIfUU&vq=small

How far in advance should a couple book their DJ?

Though it seems due to the economy there has been a lot of last minute reservations, the only true way to guarantee availability of a good DJ is to book with them well in advance. DJ reservations should be done 6-8 Months in advance.

Are all DJs required to have insurance?

No, not all venues require their vendors to have insurance, however, our opinion is that all Wedding Vendors should carry at least a One Million dollar liability policy. (This also gives you an indication on how professional your vendor is)

What type of insurance should couples check to make sure their DJs have?

At least a One Million Dollar liability policy. (This also gives you an indication on how professional your vendor is)

How far in advance of the event should the DJ arrive at the event?

The DJ should arrive no later than one hour prior to his/her start time. This should give the DJ ample time to set up, sound check, and make sure that all of the events are in order.

Are there any setup or breakdown fees that the couple is required to pay?

This varies from company to company. JAMMIN' DJs Colorado does not charge for the initial set up or tear down in most cases. The only time you will see a set up or break down cost, is if the set up/tear down requires extensive work above and beyond our normal scope.

Can couples typically request specific songs they'd like the DJ to play?

Couple should be allowed to customize their event to the music tastes they like. One thing for them to keep in mind, give your entertainer the ability to take guest requests and also play songs that they know works, after all, you are hiring them to entertain your guests.

If the answer to this is yes, how and when should these requests be made by the couple?

This again will vary from company to company. JAMMIN' DJs offers our clients the ability to complete all planning forms including the Music Request List online. We also offer a "Guest Request List" that guests can be given a link to our planning forms and make requests prior to the event.

Do Disc Jockeys usually play requests made by the guests? If yes, how is this typically done?

We accommodate guest requests in two ways. The first is by having an extensive playlist. We also offer a "Guest Request List" that guests can be given a link to our planning forms and make requests prior to the event.

Can couples request specific songs that they don't want played at their wedding? If yes, how is this handled?

Absolutely! Again, we want our clients to love their event, and if they we are playing songs they don't want to hear, we are not doing our job. They can provide an unlimited amount of "Do Not Play" songs on the online music request forms that we provide.

What are some extra services that a couple can add on to their wedding packages?

Other services that couples can add on include Up-Lighting/Decor Lights, Intelligent Lighting, Video Montage/Video Production, Event Planning Assistance, Video Projector/Screen Rental, Wedding Ceremony Service and Karaoke. These are just a few of the upgrades we offer.

How can a couple see a DJ "in action" at an event, prior to deciding whether or not to hire them?

This can be difficult at times as JAMMIN' DJs does not allow outside guests to any of our private events. We do not want to turn another person's wedding into a business showroom. However, we do have a demo video, plenty of pictures, and not to mention at least 100 references online at all times. We are also currently in the process of recording some new footage.

What if the DJ's equipment breaks during the wedding?

JAMMIN' DJs always has back up equipment at each event to prepare for the worse. If needed, we also have standby back up equipment at our office as well.

How does it work with deposits?

Specifically, how much should a couple place down for a deposit and when is the balance due?

This will vary from company to company as well. We require a small deposit that is credited towards the couples end balance. Our final balance is due 30 days prior to the event. If the event needs to be cancelled or re-scheduled, when is the latest that the couple should notify the DJ? Our contract requires our clients to notify us no later than 90 days prior to the event to have no further contractual obligations. We do make hardship exceptions for military personal and other family emergencies.

What should a couple pay attention to when interviewing DJs for their big day?

Personality, Professionalism, Equipment, and References.

Is it extra for the DJ to also act as the MC/Master of Ceremonies?

Some companies may charge for this, but we do not.

How does a couple let the "Master of Ceremonies" know what needs to be said at their wedding?

We have an extensive online planning form that our clients fill out that will cover everything from the introductions to the last dance. We then do a final consultation with the assigned DJ 30 days before their event to ensure we have all of their wishes fulfilled.

JAMMIN' DJs - Colorado
Phone: (303) 308-9700
Email: john@myjammindjs.com
Website: www.myjammindjs.com
Mailing Address: P.O. Box 2670, Denver, CO 80201

Notes

CHAPTER 8

Finding the Right Hairstylist for Your Big Day
Professional Hairstylist Terilynn of "TL Touches"

About Terilynn:

I am an independent contractor who travels for wedding services. I am the brides hair partner for the two months prior to her wedding making sure her hair is in the perfect condition for her big day, may it be with me or her regular stylist to make sure her chemical services are updated in a timely fashion to look her best.

Can a bride-to-be usually schedule a consultation session prior to her "big day" appointment?

Yes I suggest two consultation sessions

How far in advance should a bride-to-be book her appointment?

At least 6 months in advance, if not more.

Should a bride-to-be always have a "trial" session, so that she can see what her hair will look like before her wedding?

Are there situations where a trial would not be needed?

I always do trial runs, just because she likes the look in a book, doesn't mean she will like the look on mirror!!! Simple loose curls would not need a trial.

How does a trial typically work?

A trial is a few different services.

1. A nonpaid trial is not a complete up do... it is not perfected or smoothed out. Gives the bride a "general idea" of how the hair will look.

2. A paid trial is the exact hair style that the bride has chosen. Walking out with her hair in that style. An additional charge is added to remove and restyle the hair.

How long does a bride-to-be's hair need to be in order for her to wear it up?

Shoulder length. I can work magic with short hair to make it look full and beautiful.

Are there certain hairstyles that are more popular than others for the "big day"?

Side buns have been very popular lately

What types of accessories can be used in a wedding hairstyle?

Broaches, feathers, pearls, ribbons, you name it we can some how incorporate it into the hair.

Should a bride-to-be wash her hair before arriving for her appointment?

NO! I have dry shampoo. The hair will stay better if it is not washed for 24 hours.

The bride can bathe or shower, JUST DO NOT SHAMPOO THE HAIR!

What other related services can be provided to a bride-to-be?

I offer Waxing, coloring, cutting, typical salon services.

What should a bride do if it rains on her wedding day, if it's windy, or if there are other forms of bad weather?

If it is raining bring at least two umbrellas to cover you/your dress and everything in between. I always do two different styles on brides one is her "dream" look and the other is her back up look. Depending on these weather conditions that can be easily maintained by her or anyone in the wedding party if I am not on hand.

Should a bride-to-be take anything into consideration, with regard to the hairstyle she selects for different times of year / different seasons?

The humidity is a big thing. Do you really want some afro caused by it or if you wear it down, do you want it to be a ball of sweat? I go through and discuss all of these options.

What should a bride-to-be do for her hair, in the days and weeks leading up to her wedding?

I suggest no later than two weeks prior to the wedding that all chemical services be done. If these services are done with a stylist that you have been seeing regularly, then one week should be ok. Give some time for any fixes to be made, such as highlights too light or too dark, there is a line of demarcation.

Please tell us how readers can get in contact with you here:

TL TOUCHES with Beautiful Illusions Artistry (585)447-3090

CHAPTER 9

Choosing an Experienced Makeup Artist

Featuring an Interview with Melissa of "Beautiful Illusions Artistry"

Beautiful Illusions Artistry is a full-service on location makeup artistry for any special occasion! I have worked both Nationally and Internationally with Models, Photographers, Brides, and Women from all walks of life who simply desire to feel beautiful!

Does the entire bridal party normally use the services of the makeup artist too?

Yes, usually they do. Sometimes the bride chooses to pay for the girls as part of the attendant's gift, and sometimes the girls pay for themselves.

How long does the whole process take?

A full makeup application usually takes about 20 minutes.

Is it best for the bride-to-be to have her hair done first, before the makeup, or the other way around?

I advise brides to have hair done prior to makeup for a few reasons;

Please explain why it's best for one to be done before the other.

If the stylist is wetting the hair, she can often rinse away some of the makeup from the hairline in the process. Also, most brides go to a salon to have hair done, and it is nice for them to go there, then come back and be able to relax and have fun with their family and friends while waiting to get dressed and begin their special day!

How do makeup artists work with clients who have sensitive skin and various skin types?

These are concerns that the client and I address at the consultation, when I can recommend a proper skin-care regime to get her glowing for her big day!

Will makeup typically be used that has been used on other clients?

No. My kit has supplies in it, of course, however, application is always done with brushes that are sanitized between every client as well as disposable implements such as sponges, and mascara wands.

What sanitary factors should a bride-to-be ask about when speaking with makeup artists?

Ask the obvious! It's YOUR health! Ask about sanitizing practices...does the artist use hand sanitizer? Disposable implements? Antimicrobial brush cleaner? Alcohol? Most will be happy you asked, and will gladly show you their process.

What is airbrush makeup?

Airbrush makeup is liquefied pigments, micronized and applied to the skin in a micro-fine mist with the use of a gun, or "airbrush".

This makeup is usually waterproof, and paramedical grade, great for covering larger areas, tattoo and scar cover-ups, or correcting birthmarks.

Is it a good idea for a bride to wear lashes on her special day if she's not used to them? Why or why not?

YES! Nothing makes a girl feel more princes like than a nice set of wispy lashes! In addition, they help to make your eyes more noticeable in the photographs!

What are the best types of makeup products for a bride to wear on the big day?

Filled in eyebrows are a MUST! Foundation and concealer without SPF are also on the must-have list! Mascara, mascara, mascara...did I mention mascara???

And lipgloss, at the very least. Even if you were on a deserted island you would need these few little essentials!

When a bride uses a makeup artist, will she look too "overdone"?

Again, this depends on the "artist". Some are more talented than others...some have more experience with photographers, and thereby know how things look different through the camera lens. Will she "look" overdone or "feel" overdone? Depends on the girl! I have had girls squeal with absolute delight when they look in the mirror at the end of the trial...I have also had the girl who has never filled her eyebrows in or worn eyeliner emerge from the bathroom looking somewhat baffled...until I take her picture :) She then is able to see how the camera interprets things differently, and in order to not get lost in the photographs, you typically need a little bit more makeup for your big day than you would normally wear to work or the grocery store on an average day. THIS IS NOT AN AVERAGE DAY!

How does a makeup artist ensure that the bride looks good on her big day, both in person, and in photos too?

By doing a trial, and taking pictures, of course! Have your camera on standby!

What factors and options usually determine how much a makeup artist charges?

Experience, product quality, application techniques (ie. airbrush) length in the industry and extra services, such as brow design and false eyelash application can all have a bearing on price. Some artists may have special wedding packages, so always ask!

Do most makeup artists do pre-wedding consultations with the bride-to-be and the wedding party? If so, what is typically discussed at a consultation?

Yes, most do. I ask the bride to show me pictures of different looks she likes, ask her to describe to me the way she imagines herself looking and feeling on her wedding day, and then I do my best to translate that into her dream look! We also discuss how to care for her skin, how to properly shape her brows, and whether or not she will choose false lashes for that day. At the end, we discuss the date and location the makeup will be done, how many in her party will be getting makeup, and who will be responsible for payment.

Should the bride-to-be and the bridal party hire the makeup artist for a trial run first?

Absolutely! A trial is a MUST for the bride! I offer my brides a free trial as part of their package. The attendant usually do not require a prior consult unless they have a specific issue that needs to be addressed beforehand, such as a birthmark, sensitive skin or tattoo cover-up.

How far in advance should a bride-to-be book a makeup artist?

Most artists book about a year in advance...sometimes 18 months! Calendars fill up quickly, so you should secure your artist when you secure your venue and photographer!

Does the makeup artist typically come to the bride-to-be, or does the bride-to-be travel to the makeup artist?

It varies. Some brides enjoy the convenience of an on-site service, meaning the artist will go to a location of your choosing, while others don't mind taking the time to travel to a studio. Whats important is that you are confident in your artist!

Does the bride-to-be usually need to have special equipment such as special chairs, lighting, or mirrors for the makeup artist?

No, usually the artist will have everything they need. Remember...that's THEIR job!

www.beautiful-illusions.com
email: bellaillusione1@aol.com
cell: 585-748-6064

Notes

CHAPTER 10

Honeymoon Travel Booking! A Vacation That Should Never Be Forgotten!

An Interview with Jennifer of Award Winning "Sand & Sun Vacations" that specializes in Honeymoons, Destination weddings and Romance Travel.

Sand & Sun Vacations specializes in Honeymoons. Destination weddings and Romance Travel.

Winning & being nominated since 2008 numerous awards, such as Best of the Best with Travel Impressions and Sandals Resorts, Best of weddings –The Knot!

No other travel agency is so dedicated to two people in love!

From the Intimate to the Elaborate, from Romance to Adventure- your Personal Travel Consultant will listen to your every need & desire in order to customize the perfect travel experience just for the two of you! You will have someone by your side, looking out for your interest, from the moment you begin the planning process, until you return home.

Our friendly travel consultants not only have completed comprehensive educational programs but they experience, first hand, the destinations and resorts that they specialize in. They are the Experts!

*   *Personalized consultations.*
*   *Customized itineraries.*
*   *Detailed resort recommendations- photo's and critiques.*
*   *Support before, during and after your travels.*
*   *Introductory VIP letters to the general managers of the resort informing them of your Honeymoon/Destination Wedding and/or VIP status.*

By entrusting your travel plans to Sand & Sun Vacations you can be assured that our Professional Travel consultants are dedicated to providing extremely high-quality and personalized service.

Ensuring that your vacation planning is stress free. The only thing you'll need to think of is each other!

Travel Impression - Best of the Best Crystal Awards Winner- 2010, 2011

Sandals & Beaches Resorts - Best of the Best- 2010, 2011

The Knot - Best Of Weddings 2011

Sandals & Beaches Resorts Chairman's Choice Award - 2011

Why do you suggest certain resorts or destinations over others?

By reviewing your answers in our honeymoon questionnaire, asking the right questions during our consultation and listening closely, we are able to provide our clients recommendations that fit with their wants & desires- within their budgets.

In addition to the recommendations we provide our clients with a thorough review of the resort and photo's. To be sure that I have found the right resort for your vacation and budget I base my recommendations on:

A)- Site inspections done personally by us. We travel to the most popular destinations at least twice a year - more if we can! We meet with management, inspect the property and sample local attractions. We also attend training conferences, webinars and trade shows to keep up to date on resorts, management and up & coming destinations.

B) - Recent consumer reviews and information that we get through trade journals and/or fellow travel agents. There may have been a recent refurbishment or a change in management or policy since our last visit that can greatly affect the operation and moral of the resort.

C) - Reputation of the company (i.e. Sandals wins numerous awards for their properties).

This is our personalized service for you and why it's to your benefit to use our travel consultants! It may take us a tad longer to provide a quote but you can be assured that it was thoroughly researched and found to be the best vacation package for you.

We recognize that each of our clients has different needs, wants and desires- what we recommend for you may be completely different from what we recommend to the next couple!

What about all of those great last minute deals—shouldn't I wait to get the best price?

This last year has been quite a roller coaster in terms of travel & pricing - prior to the recession, travel was at its highest levels since prior to 2001. 2009 and early 2010 has seen some destinations have amazing deals and also rock bottom pricing at the last minute. However, there is a definite down side as the airlines have cut capacity, meaning that there are fewer flights available and very few non-stops. To grab the best flights we still recommend booking early as the last minute flights tend to have long layovers and lousy itineraries!

A few trends to take note of - The top suites are selling out very early- so if you are planning on booking a swim up room, oceanfront, plunge pool or other top of the line suite we highly recommend doing it early!

Travel requests and bookings are picking up across the board for all destinations, many are spurned on by great prices, value added offers such as resort and/or spa credits and people are just ready to travel and get away from the stress of everyday life ! This is causing pricing to steadily rise so those last minute deals may again disappear.

So, how can we get a deal?

Early booking discounts still offer great savings. Flexibility on traveling dates will also help you find the best price. Some suppliers will offer a vacation protection plan, for a fee, that if the price goes down you will be refunded the difference. And last but not least—package discounts! Many suppliers offer great pricing when you purchase your air & accommodations together and may even through in a few bonus amenities!

Anything that we should look out for?

Be vigilant about any offers that seem too good to be true, rock bottom pricing and any company that is willing to undercut its pricing-in these tough economic times it may be a company's last gasp effort to make a cash grab before closing its doors. Companies that prefer cash or checks may be another warning sign. Please keep in mind that some companies overseas have always done business that way, so as a consumer you really need to do your homework to see if it is a new policy or a standard.

Where do you recommend for us to go for our honeymoon/destination wedding/anniversary vacation?

There are so many amazing destinations and resorts please contact us and let us get to work finding the perfect gem for you! We'd love to discuss what you & your loved one desire for your perfect vacation and find you the best vacation package!

Warmest Regards-

Sand & Sun Vacations Travel Consultant Team

Where are the most popular honeymoon destinations?

The most popular honeymoon destinations year after year are: Mexico (particularly Riviera Maya, Puerto Vallarta & Cabo San Lucas), Jamaica, Dominican Republic, Hawaii, the Bahamas, French Poynesian Islands, Italy, and St. Lucia. Up & coming destinations are Costa Rica, Belize and Latin America.

What is the average price of a honeymoon?

For a 7 night honeymoon, with flights, average is $4800 (typically range between $3800-7000).

The average price can vary greatly due to the destination chosen, when the couple travels (in high season or off season) how far in advance a couple reserves their travel arrangements, accommodations reserved and the cost of airfare. A 4 star Tahiti honeymoon for 7 nights could easily start at over 7000, while a Jamaican, adult only, all inclusive honeymoon for 7 nights could start at 3400.00 if booked early enough.

Can a couple be married at their honeymoon destination?

In most destinations a couple can get married, there are a few exceptions because of residency requirements. Couples should be aware that there are very few destinations where they can just show up and be married without prior arrangements! How does this get arranged? If the wedding is at a resort, the travel agent can assist, in conjunction with the resort wedding coordinator, with setting the date & time, reviewing packages and informing the couple about the residence requirements, official documentation ect.. However if the couple prefers to get married outside of the resort or at a boutique resort that does not have a wedding coordinator the couple would need to hire a wedding coordinator in the destination. In many destinations the travel agent would be able to make recommendations.

I highly recommend that the couple seek the services of a travel agent that specializes in destination weddings! The details and set of skills are quite different from normal travel consulting & booking. The couple should be sure to get recommendations from other destination wedding brides or ask the travel consultant they are considering for references. There are forums dedicated to honeymoons & destination weddings such as Fabs! www.All-Inclusivebride.com where couples can chat with other destination wedding couples or read reviews!

How do cruise and land resort honeymoons differ?

While they are both amazing experiences, a cruise is great for those who enjoy being with lots of people and prefer non-stop action. They are great to provide a snapshot of many different destinations in a short period of time! However, we caution couples that a cruise is not all inclusive and to check your ship board account often! There are many extra charges not included in the cruise price that a couple may not be aware of, such as gratuities (many cruise lines add a per person, per day gratuity charge starting at $9.75), there are transfer costs to between the airport & cruise ship, soda, bottled water, alcoholic drinks and beer are all at bar prices usually with a 20% gratuity already added in, only coffee, lemonade and tea are included in the cruise fare. Many activities on the ship are at a surcharge, as are some specialty restaurants and typically each time the couple leaves the ship for an on shore excursion it cost between $50-$150 per person.

I believe land honeymoons offer a more relaxed and romantic honeymoon with the option of leaving the resort for tours or excursions. For resort honeymoons a couple has several choices- each offering a different experience- the most popular is an all-inclusive honeymoon! I have attached an article on all –inclusive, "What's To Know" that should assist with those details! The best feature o an all-inclusive is that couples have a very good idea of what the honeymoon will cost- no surprises! That makes it much more enjoyable and relaxing! All-Inclusives are found primarily in Mexico & the most popular Caribbean islands.

A couple can also do an Inclusive honeymoon- these also vary by destination & resort but typically include a choice of meal plans- some may included beverages with meals (most do not however), and may include some entertainment or activities at the resort such as the Royal Lahaina in Maui. Honeymooners will find that most resorts in Tahiti offer an inclusive package!

And then there are EP resorts- these only include your accommodations. Quite often they will also have extraneous charges for items such as parking, resort fees, may charge for coffee in room (such as at the Fiesta Americana Coral Resort in Cancun, they charged 3.00 for the in room coffee that you make yourself).

Should a couple specify that they are booking a honeymoon while making reservations? Definitely! If yes, why?

Many resorts offer amenities or acknowledgements to honeymooners! But to receive those amenities sometimes they need to provide proof prior to arrival or upon check in. Without knowing that the couples are honeymooners they will not be properly advised and may not receive those amenities! Secrets Maroma in Riviera Maya Mexico has a welcome banner that they put across the couples door stating "Honeymooners" in addition to their honeymoon package. Sandals Resorts offer honeymoon amenities but the couple must send a copy of their wedding invitation or marriage license at least a week prior to travel in order to receive!

What are some unusual and unique honeymoon destinations?

The majority of Honeymooners prefer sun & sand however honeymooners travel all over the world! The Canadian Rocky Mountains, African safaris, Machu Pichu, Galapagos, Philippines and a new travel trend of volunteerism honeymoons- where couples travel to remote destinations, or destinations ravage by natural or manmade disasters and help the local villagers with clean up, building homes, establishing schools, building wells or health related issues!

If a couple seeks an unusual honeymoon but don't wish to travel as far they can also look for unique accommodations such as underwater hotels, swim up suites such at Excellence Riviera Cancun, private bungalows like at Kona Village resort or Sandals Grande St. Lucian (complete with a private hot tub and plunge pool), treetop suites such as Sunset at The Palms, open air rain showers like at El Dorado resorts, private plunge pools such as at Regency La Toc (there are plunge pools on the cliffs with amazing views!), open air suites such as at Ladera, or open air suites with their own infinity pool such as at Jade mountain and the Millionaire Suites at Sandals Regency la Toc just to name a few!

How should a couple prepare so that their trip goes well?

Use a honeymoon travel consultant, they can best advise where to stay based on the couples preferences and desires, popular activities and things to watch out for! At Sand & Sun Vacations we provide a list of traveler tips & tricks to all of our clients! Read up on their destination prior to travel, keep an open mind and be respectful to other cultures and customs. Remember the rules in kindergarten- be polite, wait your turn and say thank you! Be prepared that English may be a second language, that food will likely be different and keep your sense of humor! Pack lightly!

They should get their passport early!

Purchase good, comprehensive travel insurance! While preparation goes a long way, you never know when something may go wrong and you will have peace of mind knowing that your financial investment or additional expenses will be reimbursed in case something goes wrong! We've had clients that needed to cancel due to the death or sickness of an immediate family member, pregnancy, a case where the groom had a seizure on his wedding night, a natural disaster in the destination, bad weather at the home airport cancelling flights, clients have been reimbursed for medical expenses incurred while at the resort the list goes on and on! Keep in mind though that not all travel policies are created equal!

What is an "adventure honeymoon package"? Typically adventure honeymoons center around a particular high energy activity such as hiking strenuous trails, bicycling, scuba diving, white water rafting/kayaking and for those very adventurous, extreme sports or an African safari.

Many couples chose to incorporate a little adventure into their honeymoon with activities such as zip lines, light hiking, swimming in cenotes, parasailing and scuba diving to name a few popular activities.

What should a couple bring with them on a honeymoon cruise? Money, money, money! Kidding aside, all the typical items that one would bring on a land based vacation to the same destination plus Dramamine (or your preferred motion sickness medicine). While must couples will never need it, it's always better to be prepared! Also inform yourselves about what each destination where the ship stops offers, and remember that a cruise is typically just a brief snapshot of a destination. Quite often the locals know they have you for only a few brief hours and selling items or services to cruise ship passengers is how they make their living, so many locals can be quite aggressive trying to get you to buy. I have found the opposite to be true when you are doing a land based vacation in the same destination- the locals tend to be charming and relaxed!

What are some of the best vacation destinations for honeymooners? There is no one size fits all honeymoon as each couple is unique and their honeymoon should reflect that! The best vacation destination is the one where they have a great time based on their needs, desires and budget! That being said the most popular destinations do tend to cater to the needs that the majority of honeymooners express! Tahiti, Mexico, Jamaica, Dominican Republic,

Hawaii, Italy, St. Lucia and the up & coming destinations of Costa Rica, Belize and Latin America.

What does the term "destination wedding" actually mean? A wedding in a destination that the couple must travel to usually outside of the state or country that the couple resides in. Most couples invite their family and friends to attend

How does a couple plan for their honeymoon?

Please see attached article *"Stress-free Honeymoon Planning Checklist"*

What is a "mini moon"?

Usually a honeymoon that only last a few days and is taken local to the couple. We find couples take mini –moons for a variety of reasons, school, work, children, financial reasons or that they wish to "honeymoon" when it's cold & snowy at home, ie a June wedding in Michigan - January or February honeymoon! We are seeing a definite trend towards taking later honeymoons in the Midwest and northeast! Most couples do end up taking a full honeymoon but at a later date.

How far in advance should a couple book their honeymoon?

We always recommend booking, if at all possible, at least 8 months out to get the best deals!
Many resorts offer early booking pricing, plus the couples have a better chance of getting the better room categories! With a travel agent a couple can deposit on the accommodations and usually round-trip transfers between

the destination airport and resort, with as little as $300.00 per couple.

Airfare, available at the 330 day mark, must be paid in full at time of booking, but can be added to the reservation at any point in time!

When should we start planning our Vacation, Destination Wedding or Honeymoon?

This pertains to any vacation package. Ideally one should start to plan at least 8 months from when they plan to travel. It'll give you plenty of time to work with our travel consultants while the best prices, flight itineraries and accommodations are available! Don't fret if your not a planner though- our travel consultants will work with you no matter how close in to date of travel you are to find the best value.

However if your plans fall on a holiday such as over Christmas, Presidents day or one of the local island celebrations or festivals you may want to plan as early as a year. Keep in mind you may not be able to get pricing until 8-10 months before your desired date, but if you are ready to deposit as soon as pricing is released you will be guaranteed the date and room category that you want! These dates are at a premium and unfortunately you will generally pay premium price!

Destination weddings are increasing in popularity and many resorts will allow you to lock in your wedding date 18 months prior to travel. We highly recommend doing so if you are very set on a date as we are seeing many prime wedding dates go quickly!

Please see attached *"Stress free Honeymoon planning checklist"* for additional notes!

What should a couple look for in a travel agent?

Someone who knows the destinations and resorts very well and preferably has been to them; someone who listens to what they want and provides the information to make the right choice.

Experience- both with honeymoons and with the destination resort- look for a travel agent that actually travels!

Listening skills- a travel agent should be asking about what you & your fiancé envision for your honeymoon- ranging from ambiance- quiet or active resort, what room category you prefer, are you beach or pool people, where you travelled previously- what did and didn't you like?, including questions regarding activities the couple may wish to participate in while on their honeymoon!

The travel agent should make recommendations based on the couples answers and letting the couple know why they are recommending the destination & resort for your honeymoon. A good travel agent will also let you know of any "quirks" you might encounter! Such as topless sunbathing, resort fees, ect!

 Be careful of travel agents that insist on a resort or destination just because they loved it if they can't explain why, based on your answers that you would love it to!!

And as with any other professional you would hire for your wedding- get referrals! Make sure that the travel agent is reputable. And remember, if something looks too good to be true it probably is!

Please see attached article "Travel Agents, Fees and Retainers" for additional information.

What are the standard/customary tips and gratuities that are paid on a honeymoon?

A couple can plan on tipping anyone who handles their luggage, drivers, tour guides, wait & bar staff, concierge, butler, maid staff, for spa services and room service.

Please keep in mind that at some all inclusive resorts tips & gratuities are included.

As an example, at Sandals Resorts gratuities at the resort are only allowed for butler service and spa services, employees can get dismissed for soliciting or accepting tips! While at the all-inclusive Royal Hideaway Play-a-car, tipping and gratuities are not expected but it is left up to your discretion. At certain all-inclusives, tipping is stated to be included but you will find the staff expecting tips and catering to the guests providing tips. Consult your travel agent for specific details for the resort that you are staying at!

Sand & Sun Vacations
Jennifer Prymula
Cherie Peninger
www.SandnSunVacations.com
Romance@SandnSunVacations.com
877-208-6639

NOTES

All-Inclusive Resort Vacations: What's to Know?
By Jennifer Prymula
Jennifer@SandnSunVacations

All-inclusive vacations are the hot ticket these days. They offer a resort experience chockfull of amenities and activities -- all for one price upfront. In some cases, everything from transportation to tips are included, so you know exactly how much your vacation will cost before you even arrive. This is especially nice for newlyweds, who have better things to do on their vacation than count pennies and balance their checkbooks.

But are "all-inclusive" vacations *really* all inclusive? In fact, the "all" part of the all-inclusive vacation can vary widely from one resort to another. Each property determines the features included in its packages, and many websites offer "all-inclusive" deals that in fact include only air transportation, transfers and accommodations. Whether it's from well meaning friends and relatives or from websites that don't tell the whole story, a couple can arrive at their all inclusive resort to find that many of the items that they assumed would be included- aren't! I've been to dozens of all inclusive resorts and no two were alike. In my experience it pays to look before you leap.

Here is what can you expect from a typical all-inclusive package. Accommodations -Yes, your lodging is included in the package, but the price will depend on such things as the size and location of the room (e.g., garden, ocean-view or beachfront) and any special features such as a hot tub, plunge pool or butler service. Things to be careful of with booking your room include whether the resort utilizes a

towel card system (lost towels can incur hefty charges), a fee for
use of the in room safe, resort fee's and if there is a complimentary mini bar, how often it is stocked and with what beverages for the All- Inclusive price. Some resorts may also charge extra for special requests, like afternoon housekeeping service on those days you want to sleep in.

Dining - Most all-inclusive resorts include meals. Some have a buffet for all meals and others have several a la carte restaurants and/or snack bars for you to choose from. These venues usually include Asian, Mexican, gourmet and Italian cuisines.
Generally speaking, the larger the resort, the more options there will be for dining.

The quality of the food can make or break a vacation – even a honeymoon – so make sure the resort offers the kind of food that makes you happy. After all, no amount of champagne and caviar is going to satisfy you if what you really want is a burger and fries. And don't be surprised to find that if the majority of guests are European that the food choices cater to their taste buds! I once was very disappointed that at an all- inclusive resort I stayed at in Jamaica did not offer jerk chicken but did have a wide variety of British food!

Three things to ask:

• Does the all-inclusive package allow dining at *any* of the resort's restaurants or are your choices limited by, say, the length of your stay or your room category?

• Is room service included in the package? If yes, is it available 24 hours a day or only during specified hours?

• Are gourmet foods and specialty dishes (like vegetarian and low-carb meals) included in the package? If not, can they be purchased for a fee?

Bar service- All beverages, including beer, wine, and cocktails, are usually available free of charge, but your selection may be limited. Some resorts serve only a small selection of domestic brands; others may offer premium brands with the package or at an additional charge. If you care what you drink, or you want a celebratory glass of champagne every night, check to see whether it is included.

Sports activities - Tennis, volleyball and fitness-center facilities are almost always included in all-inclusive packages, and most all-inclusive beach resorts offer non-motorized water-sports like windsurfing, kayaking, snorkeling, water trykes and sailing free of charge. Of course, the beach offerings depend on the beachfront. If a resort is located in an area that typically has rough water, watersports may be restricted some or all of the time (generally, red flags are raised when an activity is prohibited). There may be other restrictions, as well. Some resorts require an orientation before you can use the equipment, others have a time limit; some also require a refundable cash deposit. Expect to pay extra for pricier sporting activities like golf, horseback riding, Jet-Skiing, parasailing, and offshore fishing and scuba diving.

Entertainment - Many all-inclusive resorts include entertainment – everything from hilarious group games organized by the staff to laid-back music performed by a saxophonist during dinner. Many all-inclusive resorts have an onsite disco; admission is usually free and most include

drinks. Depending on the destination, there may be an onsite casino; drinks may or may not be included.
One thing comes included with every resort -- whether you want it or not – and that's the resort's ambience. That ambience can make or break a honeymoon, so pay careful attention to it. Does the resort cater to families, spring breakers or people within your age group? Is the resort for adults only? Is there a big singles crowd? Be very thorough with your research, and try to picture whether the property is suited to your honeymoon dream – whether that is a romantic getaway or a rollicking good time.

Weddings - As part of an All-Inclusive package a wedding may be free and include a coordinator, a few photos, flowers, champagne, music and a wedding cake. These packages usually require that you pay the government /administrative fees. Of course you can always upgrade the package to make it more personalized!

What else should you look for? Other items that may or may not be included: transportation to and from the resort, local sightseeing and excursions outside the resort, spa facilities, Internet service or wireless Internet access, gratuities, and taxes. Spa treatments are usually available for an additional fee. Some resorts will include transportation to nearby "sister properties," along with food, beverages, and use of all facilities. A few resorts may offer excursions outside the resort or greens fees at local golf courses in their package!

Start with a dream, then make a plan. Honeymoon planning can be overwhelming. It helps to sit down with your fiancee and discuss what each of you envisions for the honeymoon. Identify what features are important to you and what isn't important at all. Keep your expectations realistic to what fits within your budget. Then look carefully at each all-inclusive package and see if it offers what you are looking for. If it doesn't, move onto the next package. After all, no all-inclusive package is truly wonderful unless suits *your* needs.

Two more pieces of advice:

• First, remember the old adage: "You get what you pay for." Resorts don't give their services away – not even to happy honeymooners, so if an all-inclusive package looks too good to be true, you should be on the lookout for hidden costs and fees. Don't be afraid to ask *exactly* what is included and how much the "extras" will cost.

• Second, consider working with a travel professional that specializes in honeymoons. Generally, using a travel agent will cost the same if not less than booking on the internet however you will gain the expertise and knowledge of a professional. A travel professional is able to sort the information, clarify your expectations, avoid common pitfalls and know who the best supplier is for a particular resort or destination. They will know hundreds of properties – the amenities, food quality, clienteles and reputations either from personal experience or their multitude of resources and training. A good travel agent also knows how to stick to a budget – even if you don't! And here's a bonus: if something should go wrong, you have a consumer advocate on your side who has a great deal of negotiating power.

All-inclusive resort vacations are a good bet for honeymooners. Do your homework before placing your deposit and you will have a great start on your new life together.

About the author: Jennifer Prymula, is certified as a Honeymoon & Destination Wedding Specialist by The Travel Institute, Certified Sandals Specialist, Hawaii Destination Specialist and an Accredited Cruise Counselor. She is a member of the West Michigan Wedding Association and KBA.

You can contact Jennifer at: 877-208-6639; Jennifer@SandnSunVacations or visit her website at www.SandnSunVacations.com

Copyright 2007

Stress Free Honeymoon Planner

by Jennifer Prymula, Sand & Sun Vacations

Most brides and grooms spend countless hours, days, weeks and months planning for the "Big Day." Unfortunately, *honeymoon* planning often gets much less attention. And that's too bad, because the honeymoon is your chance to unwind after all the excitement of the wedding – and it's the beginning of your new life together. It should be a celebration all its own, not an afterthought! So, I've taken it upon myself to write my own "Stress-Free Honeymoon Planner." Consider it my wedding anti-stress gift to you!

9–8 months before the honeymoon

Dream, dream, dream. Start discussing what each of you wants for your dream honeymoon. You need to agree on a general theme (e.g. tropical or cosmopolitan, romantic or adventurous), then you can let your imaginations soar. It's a great way to put some snuggle time and fun into your wedding preparations!

Get out your calendar. Determine how long your honeymoon can be and schedule the time off of work. Remember that honeymoons to distant destinations like Tahiti and Fiji will require more than a week because of travel time and time zone differences. No matter where you go, be sure to plan a day or two to recuperate after you get back home.

Budget realistically. Budget realistically (ok- I agree this part isn't fun!) – you'll need to include airfare, transportation once at the destination-typically called transfers, accommodations, sightseeing, gratuities, meals and souvenirs. And starting now will mean that you don't shortchange your honeymoon by spending it all on the wedding.

Speaking of .... As you work out your budget, keep in mind that your wedding lasts but a couple of hours, while your honeymoon goes on for a week or more. Don't shortchange yourself by put all of your funds into the wedding! Which do you think you'll remember more in five years --- the centerpieces at the reception or a private candle lit dinner on the beach with your toes in the sand and the stars twinkling above and discussing your future hopes and dreams?

The unique placards for your guests or learning to snorkel together while holding hands? And don't kid yourselves that your room category doesn't matter -- you will be newlyweds after all! Believe me, hearing the waves lap against the shore, while enjoying a view of the sunset from your private plunge pool will be immensely more romantic than a room with a view (and the noise and smells) of the parking lot!

8–7 months ahead

Hire a travel agent. Contact travel agents and interview a few to see who you click with. Working with an agency that focuses on honeymoons is a great idea as they know which resorts cater to the honeymoon crowd and have the contacts to make sure that everything goes smoothly. Ask about experience, if they book travel full or part time and for references. The travel professional should ask a lot of questions about what the two of you want for your dream honeymoon before making any recommendations. Be honest about budget and expectations, then relax. The travel professional will get to work for you! Another advantage of working with a travel agent is you will not need to pay your package in full, **only a deposit**! This provides the freedom to book early and lock in early booking rates and the best rooms!

Book it! Review the options, choose a honeymoon package, then place your deposit with your travel agent and relax. That's one more thing off the wedding to do list!

Plus, as an added bonus, when the wedding plans start to get hectic, you can daydream about your fantastic honeymoon- knowing it's just waiting for the two of you! Don't forget to purchase travel insurance!

So what if you're already past the 8-7 month mark- don't fret! Use a great travel agent and they'll get you the best options and pricing available!!

6 months ahead

Get your travel documents in order. If you don't already have a passport, apply for one now (yes, if there are

complications it can take months for your passport to
arrive). If you do have passports, check the expiration dates
to be sure they will be valid when you travel. A good rule of
thumb is that your passport should be valid for six months
beyond your return date; in fact, some countries require this,
so check with your travel agent or visit the State Department
Web site at www.travel.state.gov. Also check to see if you will
need any visas and shots. If there are back child support
issues-now is the time to clear them up-before you apply for
a passport!

3 months ahead

Review current luggage requirements. Check the
luggage you have available against your airline's luggage
requirements. You will need to check both size and weight
limits.
Airline rules are strict, so borrow or buy new luggage if you
have to. Also check special TSA requirements concerning
locks, contraband and carry-on restrictions. Currently the
rules state that each person can only carryon liquids and gels
if they are in their original 3 oz. or less container and all of
your liquids & gels must fit in a clear, quart-size, zip-top bag
-- so, no, you won't be bringing that magnum of champagne
aboard. There are no restrictions currently about liquids in
your checked luggage.

Dress for success. If you have any questions about the
dress expectations at your honeymoon destination, contact
your travel agent. Be sure to bring a sweater or light jacket
(planes and air conditioning can get quite chilly), along with
sturdy shoes for that long romantic walk on the beach and

for sightseeing. If you plan to go horseback riding, you'll need a pair of blue jeans as well as those shoes mentioned above (no sandals). I recommend at least two swim suits for both men and women. Swimsuits may not dry as quickly in tropical climates as they do at home, and it's uncomfortable putting on a damp swimsuit (trust me on this one!). Bring along a couple of gallon size zip top bags to transport damp swimsuits home in!

Buy sunscreen and bug repellant. Sunscreen is a must! While a nice tan can be very sexy, there is nothing romantic about sunburn! I usually bring two sunscreens: one high SPF for the first few days and then a slightly lower SPF for the rest of the week; I also pack aloe vera, which soothes sun-kissed skin. If you are traveling in the tropics, bug repellant with DEET is a high priority.

2 months ahead

Make final payment. This is as easy as calling your travel agent and saying go ahead and use the credit card on file!

Take care of the home front. Make arrangements for a house and pet sitter if you'll need them. Don't forget to have a backup plan in case these fall through. Also arrange for someone to deliver wedding gifts and keepsakes to your house from the reception, take your wedding dress to the cleaners, return any formalwear or other rentals, and otherwise take care of the wedding cleanup.

3 weeks ahead

Copy everything. Make a copy of your travel arrangements, your passports and your credit cards and leave it with a trusted family member or friend. Be sure to give them your travel agent's contact information as well.

Hold the deliveries. Unless someone can pick up your mail and newspapers every day, make arrangements to stop delivery. Nothing says "Come rob this house" like a stack of newspapers in the driveway.

Check your camera. Check that your camera is in working condition and pick up extra batteries, memory card(s) or film.

2 weeks ahead

Take out your list and get packing. Two weeks will give you enough time to pick up anything you need and still attend to all the last-minute wedding details. Be sure to pack an extra bag or bring an extra suitcase for those souvenirs and gifts you're bound to bring home.

Cross-pack. I recommend cross packing, i.e., putting half of your clothes in each other's suitcase. This way, if the airline misplaces a suitcase for a day or two, neither of you is completely out of clothes!

Consider your carry-on carefully. Pack your tickets, passports, money, personal items, and a change of clothes in your carry-on bag. Also pack your glasses and any medications, making sure they are in their original labeled bottles.

Alert financial managers. Call your bank and credit card company to let them know your travel dates and where to. This way you'll avoid your accounts being frozen for what appears to be suspicious charges! Advance notification may also provide protection if unauthorized charges show up.

The day before

Attend to last-minute details. Confirm flight schedule. Double check carryon bag.

Day of departure

Get ready for take-off. Know that the getaway can be hectic, especially if you are leaving directly from the wedding reception. There will be aunts to kiss and tin cans to remove from the back of the car, so start early. You must arrive at the airport early enough to allow for security screening; international flights generally require you to be there at least three hours before departure.

Drink up. Drink plenty of water to stay hydrated both before and during travel.

Relax and go with the flow. The wedding is over and now you can enjoy each others company!

Congratulations and have a Pina Colada for me!

About the author: Jennifer Prymula, is a certified Honeymoon & Destination Wedding Specialist, & a Preferred Sandals Resorts Specialist- with Sand & Sun Vacations being the top Sandals agency in West Michigan!

You can contact Jennifer at 269.686.0595 Jennifer@SandnSunVacations or visit her website at www.SandnSunVacations.com

Copyright 2010

Travel Agents, Retainers and Fees - Why?!

In today's world of wedding travel, honeymooners are finding that more and more specialized agencies are starting to charge upfront fees. These fees may be called by different names such as Plan To Go, Retainers, Booking fee, Research fee and so on.

Each Travel Agency is a bit different in the amount they charge, if they give it back as a resort credit, towards final payment, after travel or even at all. So what does this fee include, how much is it and is it justified?

The fee can vary widely from agency to agency-to provide a general idea I'll let you know what my agency, Sand & Sun Vacations policies are!

For my honeymooners we charge a $50 retainer and for our Destination Wedding brides it varies depending on size of the guests list but starts at $100 for groups of 5 rooms or more. The honeymoon retainer is given back after travel and half of the Destination Wedding retainer is given back after travel.

If we give it back- why do we charge it all? Basically it comes down to 3 things- Service, Time and Commitment. We will work with only a few clients at a time so that we can provide amazing service to them. We can also be assured we have the time to it takes time to fully research all of the options available and answer all of the brides and grooms (and their guests, if it's a destination wedding) questions. Because we only work with a few clients we needed a way to be sure that the brides & grooms were as committed to us as we are to them- voila the retainer!!

Sort of like paying a deposit to your wedding photographer- they have the skills, knowledge and style that you like but to secure their commitment to your date you must provide a deposit. By booking that photographer you have a peace of mind that your photos will be everything you dream of!

So how about a travel agent- what do we offer that makes paying a retainer for our commitment to you worthwhile? Again, we're all different but this is what I and many other Honeymoon & Destination Wedding Travel Consultants provide:

Skills- Honeymoon & Destination Wedding travel consultants understand that each couple is unique and enjoy different things. Travel consultants should discuss with the bride and groom what they want, desire and can budget for their travel! Using that information a good travel agent will make recommendations for a resort and destination that provides what the couple dreamt about for their honeymoon.

For Destination Weddings we ask what the couple envision for their wedding ceremony, guest accommodations and price range plus if they want to schedule any group activities. Your Destination Wedding consultant will provide one point of reference to ask questions for both the wedding couple and their guests-that way the happy couple aren't slammed with questions about the resort, the destination, passports ect! They also assist with the resorts wedding coordinator is the bride so desires.

Knowledge- Many of the Travel Consultants that specialize in Honeymoons and Destination Weddings also spend a tremendous amount of time training. Personally I devote at least several hours a day educating myself -whether I am reading up on changes at destinations and resorts in trade magazines, taking courses, meeting with a tourist board or supplier representative (and forming those relationships that benefit my clients). I also travel a couple of times a year to the properties (on my own dime- no, as TA's we do not travel for free!) to meet with general managers, wedding coordinators and to do site inspections. Most of us, even on our personal vacations spend time doing site inspections at resorts so that we are better informed for our clients!

Style-There are many extras that Travel Consultants may provide to their clients. For sand & Sun vacations Honeymooners and Destination Wedding couples we provide detailed and honest reports and photos of the resorts we recommend! In addition we provide travel & packing tips and destination reports. It's always relaxing to go to a destination and resort fully informed, and not encountering any major surprises! Plus with all that the bride & groom have to do preparing for their wedding day it's nice that they don't have to spend countless hours on the internet searching for valid and updated information!

Peace of Mind – Your Travel Consultant is there to answer all of your questions before, during and after travel. Troubleshoot any potential issues before they happen-

Travel Consultants know that often times a valid connection- one that an airline or online agency will sell –may not be a reasonable connection! Prior to booking the travel arrangements the Travel Consultants review the flights to make sure connection times are reasonable, and they may know of other issues at an airport that would make that connection difficult to make!

The Travel Consultant will service all of the travel arrangements from deposit till everyone arrives home. I've heard horror stories of bridesmaids or groomsmen that booked online and who end up calling the bride the day before the wedding because they are having flight issues and couldn't get assistance from the online agency nor the airline- the poor brides did not need that stress before their wedding! Travel Consultants will assist in getting their clients to the destination if there is an issue!

For Destination Weddings, the Travel Consultant will keep track of the guest bookings and provide a weekly or bi-monthly report of which guests have deposited and their travel dates. Having all of the guests book through one agency gives the brides and groom more time to focus on the wedding festivities!

There are additional reasons that a Travel consultant may require a retainer or fee. Most Travel Consultants, unless they are in a large agency, work on commission. This commission isn't paid till after the client travels, anywhere from 2-6 weeks after. So we basically work for our clients, dispensing advice, answering questions, providing quotes and negotiating on your behalf, taking care of any issues while our clients are traveling all without getting paid for those services- and I thought getting paid bi-weekly was tough! If the client doesn't travel due to unforeseen circumstances unfortunately the Travel Consultant isn't paid. The retainer will at least cover some of the time and expenses that were incurred.

I highly encourage honeymooners and those couples who desire a Destination Wedding to interview potential Travel Consultants, ask about fees, what services they cover and what the couple can expect. Remember that not all Travel Consultants are created equal. Ask for a contract and realize that a good travel agent is a professional who is there to make your wedding planning more enjoyable by taking care of the travel details!

About the author: Jennifer Prymula, is certified as a Honeymoon & Destination Wedding Specialist& Certified Sandals Specialist. She is a member of the West Michigan Wedding Association and Kalamazoo Bridal Association. **You can contact Jennifer at 877-208-6639;** *Jennifer@SandnSunVacations.com or visit her website at www.SandnSunVacations.com*

Copyright 2007

NOTES

CONCLUSION

Congratulations! You now have the combined knowledge that all of our interviewees have been generous enough to share! We hope that you now feel confident and excited to go out and plan your special day. Before you get started, though, we'd just like to share a little more advice with you:

In all likelihood, you're only going to have one wedding. Moreover, this also means that you're also only going to have one time in your life when you are planning your wedding. Our advice to you is to not make just the big day the only fun part. We truly hope that you enjoy the process of planning your wedding as much as you enjoy your wedding day.

We certainly hope that you find enjoyment in your wedding planning journey. We hope that you cherish each moment of planning your wedding, even if unexpected things still happen along the way. Always remember that life would be boring if everything always went exactly as expected. When unexpected things happen, try to smile and accept it as part of the journey.

We have done our best to compile the best advice that we were able to find, from true wedding industry professionals. Even though you now have a substantial advantage over couples who plan their weddings without the knowledge that you now have, there are still bound to be some bumps in the road, in the days leading up to your big day. As with all things in life, it's not what happens to you throughout the wedding planning process, it's how you handle those things that happen to you along the way. Embrace the challenges and welcome the unexpected. Each obstacle that you eliminate will take you one step closer to your special day.

We wish you all the very best while you prepare for your wedding day. May you find joy, happiness and fun throughout all the days prior to your wedding day, and beyond!

Notes

3897616R00063

Printed in Great Britain
by Amazon.co.uk, Ltd.,
Marston Gate.